AF395824

A conversation with my dad
A lesson learned

A conversation with my dad:
A lesson learned.
Jessica Doxey-Gray
Illustrated by Rida Zubairi

Xulon Press
2301 Lucien Way #415
Maitland, FL 32751
407.339.4217
www.xulonpress.com

Paperback ISBN-13: 978-1-66284-327-3
Hard Cover ISBN-13: 978-1-66284-328-0
Ebook ISBN-13: 978-1-66284-329-7

Dedication

This book is dedicated to Charles and Mary Doxey, who always taught me the priority of having a relationship with God.

When I was little, my dad always had a solution to my problems, no matter how simple the problem, he always had the same solution: to pray.

For example, one day after school,
things weren't so good.

My friends and I were playing outside, and I noticed that
the streetlights were coming on. "Oh no It's time to go
home, I sighed." "Do you really have to go home now? they
asked." My friends really didn't want me to leave because
they wanted to play one more game of hide-and-seek.

“I have to go home,” I said to them.

“Okay, we will see you at school tomorrow,” they replied.

SCHOOL

When I arrived at school the next day, I was happy to see my friends, but they ignored me. Even during recess, they wouldn't speak to me and that made me feel sad.

12

When I returned home, my mother was in the kitchen cooking dinner. I told her what happened at school and explained how it made me feel sad because I love my friends.

"It will be alright, do not worry," she said. "Your friends may not understand the importance of being on time or being obedient when your parents have rules. We all make mistakes. They will apologize no worries."

I understood but I wanted to find my dad to tell him about my problem and to share the wisdom that my mom had given me. My parents would often share godly wisdom with the family because they wanted all of us to know that God loved us, and that He had a plan for our lives if we would just draw closer to Him.

I went outside looking for my dad. He was washing the car, so I asked if it would be all right to talk with him about something.

"What's wrong?" he asked. "Are you okay?" I guess the sadness on my face gave me away.

My dad looked at me with concern as I began to sob.

"You told me I'm supposed to treat others with kindness, but my friends aren't treating me that way. That's not fair!" I cried. "Although he had been busy washing the car, he had stopped and waited patiently until I had calmed down enough to hear what he had to say."

"Sweetheart, you're the apple of God's eye, and He loves you," he said. I didn't respond because I was still feeling really sad, and suddenly really mad.

Seeing that I was still hurting, he placed his cleaning sponge down and dried his hands. "Let's talk, ladybug. I can tell that this is really bothering you."

"Okay, dad, let's talk," I said while waiting for him to finish drying his hands.

"Let's go and have a seat on the porch and talk about it," he said.

After we sat down and I shared the story about my friends, dad said, "You should show others kindness regardless of how they treat you. Sometimes people don't know how it makes others feel when they're mean. Sometimes people might be mean just because they're having a bad day."

Dad put his arm around me and said, "Baby girl, I'm not telling you to let people mistreat you. I'm telling you not to change who you are in your heart and in God. Sometimes people need others to help them along the way. That's why I always tell you and your sisters to pray. We are not perfect people, but we should try to be better and learn from our mistakes. Only God can help us change. We should show grace to all mankind. God loves us all; that's why we must pray."

After our conversation, I went to my room, and I prayed. Dear God, please do not allow my friends to be mean to me anymore. I don't believe that I was mean to them but if I was, please forgive me and I forgive them.

The next day, I headed to school with confidence in myself, knowing that I was a nice person and that I deserved having my friends treat me nicely. Most of all, I knew that God loved me, and that he heard my prayer.

And you know what? When I arrived at school, my friends apologized, and they were nice to me! Now I know for myself that this is what happens when you pray. From that day on, I had a closer relationship with God.

When I got home, I threw down my backpack, and I ran upstairs to tell dad all about my great day. I gave him a big hug and told him that I appreciated all that he had taught me.

Dad smiled back at me and said, "I love you sweetheart", I knew that God would fix everything."

I appreciate what Dad taught me so much that now I want to teach you some of his prayer lessons. I think they will help you just like they helped me. Ask your parents to explain what they mean if you don't understand and try out one of these lessons every day.

Prayer Lesson 1:

PRAYER ALWAYS WORKS according to (Mark 11:24) Therefore I tell you, whatever you ask in prayer, believe that you have received it and it shall be yours.

Prayer Lesson Example:

Find a quiet place to pray and talk to God about your problems and HE WILL answer your prayer.

Prayer Lesson 2:

PRAY without worrying according to (Jeremiah 29:12) Then you will call on me and come and pray to me, and I will listen to you.

Prayer Lesson Example:

Instead of worrying about an issue, **TRUST** God. After you're done talking to Him, believe that He heard you, and go enjoy the rest of your day.

Prayer Lesson 3:

Write your **VISION** and make it plain, according to (Habakkuk 2:2).

____

Prayer Lesson Example:

My sisters and I would often write a letter to God, seal it in an envelope, leave it in the Bible, and wait for God to answer our **PRAYER.**

I can truly say that **GOD** answers prayers. After you put these lessons into practice, you'll be saying the same, too!

God, I honor you and thank **YOU** for every opportunity that You have provided. Amen!